What's it like to be a...
TEACHER

Written by Kira Daniel
Illustrated by Diane Paterson

Troll Associates

Special Consultant: Karen Alevy, *Fourth Grade Teacher, New City, New York.*

Library of Congress Cataloging-in-Publication Data

Daniel, Kira.
    Teacher / by Kira Daniel; illustrated by Diane Paterson.
        p.   cm.—(What's it like to be a...)
    Summary: Describes the many educational, supportive, and fun
things one representative teacher does with and for the students in
his class.
    ISBN 0-8167-1430-4 (lib. bdg.)   ISBN 0-8167-1431-2 (pbk.)
    1. Teaching—Vocational guidance—Juvenile literature.
2. Elementary school teachers—Juvenile literature. [1. Teachers.
2. Occupations.] I. Paterson, Diane, 1946-   ill. II. Title.
III. Series.
LB1776.D36   1989
372.13—dc19   88-10041

10 9 8 7 6 5 4 3 2 1

933494

What's it like to be a...
TEACHER

My teacher, Mr. Benson, is not the teacher I wanted this year. I thought Mrs. Ennis with her bright red hair looked like more fun. But now I wouldn't trade for anything!

I remember that rainy day last fall. I fell in a mud puddle on my way to school. I was wet. I was cold. I felt awful. My homework was even wetter than I was. And, I forgot my lunch!

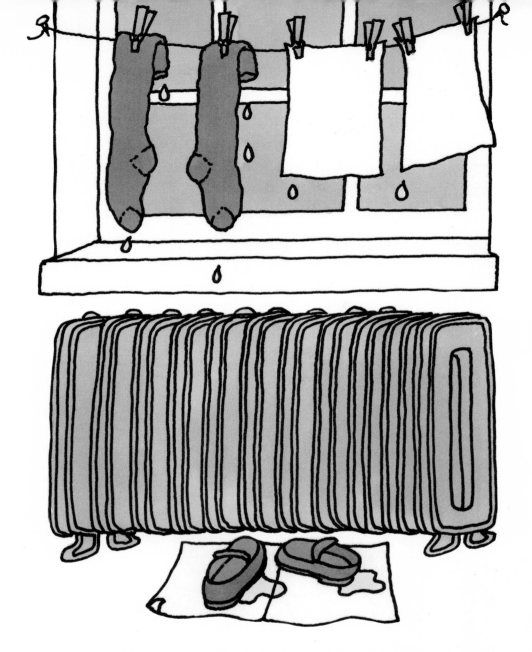

Mr. Benson knew just what to do. First, he
dried my socks and shoes near the radiator.
Next, he called my mom for dry clothes and a
peanut-butter sandwich. Then, he set out my
homework to dry, and he smiled at me.

That same day, it was my job to feed Norma, our class fish. I slipped and dropped about a gallon of fish food into the tank. Norma had a year's supply of food all at once!

"Poor Norma," I cried, as I scooped the extra food out of the tank.

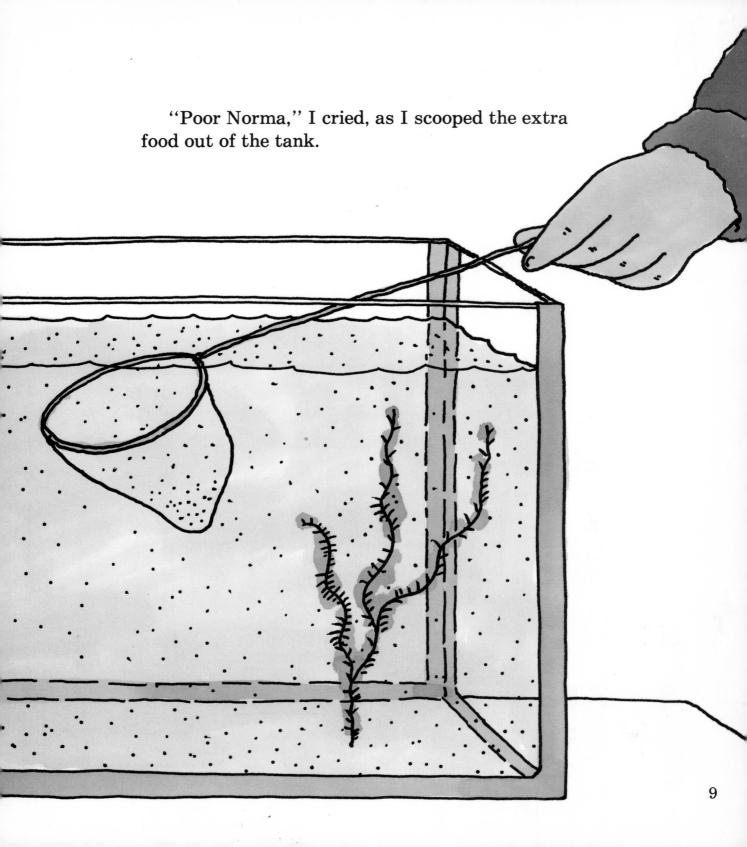

I looked at Mr. Benson. He was smiling. He put his hand on my shoulder and said, "Norma will be okay, and so will you. Tomorrow will be a better day." And he was right!

Mr. Benson does not *always* smile. Sometimes he gets angry. Like when kids keep asking him if it's lunch time when it's only 10 o'clock. Or when we don't try hard enough to do our best work.

I do *my* best work in reading and writing. Those are things I *really* enjoy. Math is a different story.

I used to hide my hands under my desk, so I could count with my fingers. I didn't want anyone to know that I needed my fingers to add and subtract. But Mr. Benson gave me beads and blocks for counting. He taught me how to think about numbers. Now math makes sense.

My teacher, Mr. Benson, gets to school early each morning. He sets up our work for the day. He puts up exciting bulletin boards. He checks his lesson plans. He meets with parents. He talks to our principal and with other teachers.

Sometimes he gives kids extra help before school. (Sometimes he helps us after school, too.)

Mr. Benson always tapes a morning puzzle to the door. It's the first thing we see when we come in. The morning puzzle is usually a tricky question. The first person with the answer is the winner. Mr. Benson says the morning puzzle makes our sleepy minds wake up! "It gives you a smart start," he says. I've won the morning puzzle nine times so far.

17

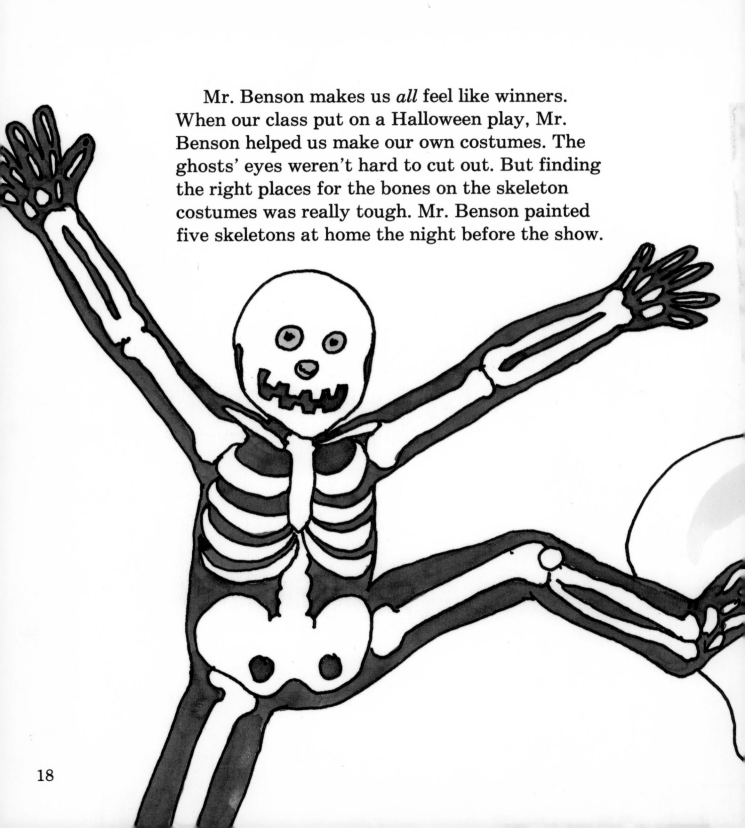

Mr. Benson makes us *all* feel like winners. When our class put on a Halloween play, Mr. Benson helped us make our own costumes. The ghosts' eyes weren't hard to cut out. But finding the right places for the bones on the skeleton costumes was really tough. Mr. Benson painted five skeletons at home the night before the show.

18

Everyone loved our play. Especially our parents!

Mr. Benson invites our parents to come and work with our class whenever they can. Every Tuesday afternoon a parent comes and reads to us. Last week my mom came. It felt great to have her there.

Once during the winter, Mr. Benson's car got stuck in the snow. He got to school really late. We thought we'd have a substitute for the whole day. But then Mr. Benson came in all covered with snow. "I'll bet you didn't expect a snowman for a teacher," he laughed. Mr. Benson shows us the bright side of just about everything!

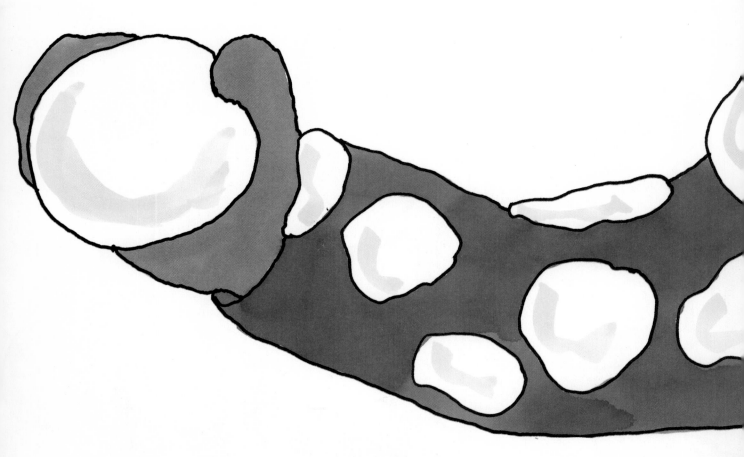

Mr. Benson works hard, checking our papers
and thinking of great projects for our class to do.
He has good ideas.

Mr. Benson showed me how to build my own exploding volcano. I made it from glue and paper. Baking soda made the volcano bubble over. My volcano was really great! Everyone said so.

In the spring, Mr. Benson brought in packs of flower seeds. We dug up the dirt outside our classroom. Then Mr. Benson showed us how to plant the seeds and water them each day. Now we look out on our very own flowers. I like the red ones best.

At the end of the day, we always write in our journals. Mr. Benson gave us notebooks on the first day of school. He told us to write down our thoughts. Or what we did that day. Or what we wished we had done. Mr. Benson started *his* journal when he was in college, learning to be a teacher. I'm going to write in *my* journal for the next hundred years!

Sometimes Mr. Benson looks really tired.
That's usually after we collect milk money. Or
take book-club orders. Or talk during a fire drill.

But most of the time, he looks bright and happy. Mr. Benson says there is no job as exciting as teaching. He says he loves seeing our faces when we learn new things.

Yes, I think Mr. Benson is the best teacher in the whole world.

Summer is coming. But I wish this year
would never end. Of course, next year's teacher,
Mrs. Star, *does* seem nice. I guess I'll just have
to wait and see.